The Wise Son

Written by Amy Norris

Illustration by Alexis Olguin & Amy Norris

There once as a boy
Whom his Father knew well
He was kind and whole-hearted
And it was easy to tell..

The boy wasn't gifted with talent
Or looks
He wasn't gifted in sports
Nor his mind full of books

But he grew up to listen
To the things he had been taught
He guarded his eyes
His life and his thoughts

He chose what was good
Each day he was given
And the Father was proud
Of this life he was livin'

One day while the boy
Was walking with God
The Lord gave him a gift
A small seed in a pod

He noticed a hole
Right there in the ground
He wanted to plant it
Where it wouldn't be found

So watering it daily
Planting it in full sun
Tending it's life
Until each day was done

The tree grew to be strong
And the boy grew to be wise

With each passing year
The tree grew to full size

He soon noticed the tree
Was full of good fruit
And good shade
He felt proud of himself
Tending the gift that God made

So he began to share
The fruit and the shade

With all of his family
And the friends he
Had made!

All over town
He was known by his deeds
And the Lord blessed him again
With more gifts and more seeds

A wife was now given
And right from the start

She gave him her life
And he gave her his heart

And he was happy with life
And the family they raised
And they lived all their lives
Under the trees in the shade

And he learned that serving God
Was serving others you see
And the Lord blessed him each day
And his whole family tree!!

Parent Guide

These are suggestions as you read this book.
It is up to you as the care giver to determine
What is right for your family

This book is intended to be read with your child.
It is a tool to help you discuss the topic of addiction.
Consider the age of the child and consider whether
or not the child is ready for subject.

Use the scriptures provided here to talk about
God's good plan for our lives and what it
Happens when we go astray

Watch for cues from your child to determine
Readiness. Give them time to talk and ask
Questions as you read

Educating your child on specific addiction
Issues early is better then damage control
Later.

Scriptures

Matthew 6:22-23New International Version (NIV)
22 "The eye is the lamp of the body. If your eyes are healthy,[a] your whole body will be full of light. 23 But if your eyes are unhealthy,[b] your whole body will be full of darkness. If then the light within you is darkness, how great is that darkness!

1st John 2:16
16 For everything in the world—the lust of the flesh, the lust of the eyes, and the pride of life—comes not from the Father but from the world.

Luke 8:17
For there is nothing hidden that will not be disclosed, and nothing concealed that will not be known or brought out into the open.

Ephesians 5:18
Don't be drunk with wine, because that will ruin your life. Instead, be filled with the Holy Spirit,

Proverbs 7:22
All at once he followed her
    like an ox going to the slaughter,
like a deer[a] stepping into a noose[b]
23
    till an arrow pierces his liver,
like a bird darting into a snare,
    little knowing it will cost him his life.

Written by Amy Norris
Illustrated by
Alexis Olguin & Amy Norris
© 2017 truthbetoldministries.com
Reservation of Rights
ISBN-13: 978-0692749456
ISBN-10: 0692749454
TBT Ministries NPO
www.trainupachildministries.com
www.truthbetoldministries.com

www.ingramcontent.com/pod-product-compliance
Lightning Source LLC
Chambersburg PA
CBHW042119040426
42449CB00002B/111